Funeral Sermons that Proclaim and Celebrate

George Reed, O.S.L.

CSS Publishing Company, Inc.
Lima, Ohio

FUNERAL SERMONS THAT PROCLAIM AN CELEBRATE

Copyright © 2020 by
CSS Publishing Company, Inc.
Lima, Ohio

All rights reserved. No part of this publication may be reproduced in any manner whatsoever without the prior permission of the publisher, except in the case of brief quotations embodied in critical articles and reviews. Inquiries should be addressed to: Permissions, CSS Publishing Company, Inc., 5450 Dixie Hwy, Lima, Ohio 45807.

Library of Congress Cataloging-in-Publication Data: Reed, George (George E.), 1948- author. Title: And the sea was no more : funeral sermons that proclaim and celebrate / George Reed, O.S.L. Description: Lima, Ohio : CSS Publishing Company, Inc., 2020. | Identifiers: LCCN 2019046857 | ISBN 9780788029837 | ISBN 9780788029844 (ebook) | ISBN 0788029835 | ISBN 0788029843 Subjects: LCSH: Funeral sermons. | Bible--Sermons. Classification: LCC BV4275 .R44 2020 | DDC 252/.1--dc23 LC record available at https://lccn.loc.gov/2019046857

For more information about CSS Publishing Company resources, visit our website at www.csspub.com or email us at csr@csspub.com or call (800) 241-4056.

ISBN-13: 978-0-7880-2983-7
ISBN-10: 0-7880-2983-5

e-book:
ISBN-13: 978-0-7880-2984-4
ISBN-10: 0-7880-2984-3   PRINTED IN USA

The book is dedicated to my maternal grandfather, The Reverend Joseph Elva Overholser, a licensed minister in The Church of the Brethren. His influence on my life has been very deep as he touched my life personally, through my mother, and through the local congregation where I began my church life.

Table Of Contents

Introduction	7
Sample Sermon Based On Psalm 23	9
The Rainbow Genesis 9:8-17	13
The Good Shepherd Psalm 23	17
A Time Ecclesiastes 3:1-15	21
Come To The Feast Isaiah 25:6-9	24
Comfort My People Isaiah 40: 1-8	27
Hope In The Midst Of Despair Isaiah 40:28-31 Psalm 23 Revelation 21:1-7 John 14	31

Come And Rest   36
    Matthew 5:3-10, 11:28-30

Jesus Walks With Us   39
    Luke 24:13-35

Many Rooms   43
    John 14:1-14, 18-19, 25-27

If God Is For Us   47
    Romans 8:31-39

Love   50
    1 Corinthians 13

God's Fullness Within Us   53
    Ephesians 3:14-21

And The Sea Was No More   56
    Revelation 21:1-7

Introduction

I have been at too many funerals where the preacher talked extensively about the person without ever offering much in the way proclaiming our faith. At other times I have sat through intense reflections on biblical texts without having heard a word about the person whose funeral I was attending. These funeral sermons are written to proclaim a biblical message that addresses the mourners while also providing a celebration of the deceased. The proclamation portion is written with a place to put personal reflections about the deceased. These sermons are meant to be used in three different ways.

The preacher can read the sermons and use bits and pieces to write their own sermon. In this way they serve as a place to start whether the sermon sparks a similar thought in the preacher or leads them to take an entirely different slant.

The sermons can also be taken as is but tweaked to better fit the style and theology of the preacher. Use what can be used and change the rest.

They can also be taken entirely as written with just the personal reflection added to make the celebration part speak to the mourners about the life they have come to grieve over and celebrate. These sermons tend to be short.

I have found that with the personal reflection added they are a good length for a funeral service. They can certainly be expanded if the need is felt.

If you read through these sermons and think, "I can do better than that" then I have done my job and I wish you well. However, you use this resource I hope that it will be helpful in the very important ministry of proclaiming God's truth while also celebrating the life of one whose departure from this life is being grieved.

Sample Sermon Based On Psalm 23

Here is an example of one of these sermons with the personal information included. Since this is an actual sermon I recently preached at a funeral, I have taken out the names.

The Good Shepherd

The image of the Good Shepherd is a much beloved one in the church. The idea that God is our shepherd who looks out for us is a reassuring and comforting one. When God is leading us there is nothing that we need besides this. God takes us to green pastures and still waters. God restores and refreshes our souls so that we know peace and joy in our lives. No matter what happens, however bad it seems, we know that God is with us to comfort us and guide us. God is generous to supply our needs and blesses us forever more. Our greatest joy is to be with God.

It is no wonder that the church took up that image with Jesus and it has become a large part of how we understand him. He is the one who leads us and watches over us. He seeks us when we are lost and he carries us in his arms of love. He is the one who leads us by the still waters where we refresh ourselves during the dry times of life. He is the one who leads us to green pastures where we are fed and strengthened for our journey. He is the one who restores our souls when life tries to tear us apart. He is the one who sets the table of banquet where we rejoice in the goodness of life and celebrate the love that surrounds us.

Each Sunday morning as we gather for worship, we celebrate the presence of the risen Christ who comes to be our Good Shepherd. In the reading of the scriptures, the hymns, prayers, sermons, sacraments, and the fellowship before or afterward, Christ is present to us. We find ourselves being refreshed and renewed for our daily lives as we spend time together in the presence of our shepherd.

He is, also, the one who walks with us through the dark valleys, even the valley of death. Today we look for the comfort in a time of darkness and loss. It is sometimes difficult to sense him in the darkness but if we listen carefully we will hear his voice of guidance and care. Sometimes that voice comes through others who speak to us. It is sometimes easier to hear the divine voice when we hear it through human words. Sometimes that love is most evident to us when we can see it in action through flesh and blood.

So today we gather to share our love and our stories with one another. We come to hear the voice of the Good Shepherd reflected in the voices of family and friends. We cry together and we laugh together and we know that in both we are embraced in the arms of our loving God. Today we share more than the time in the dark valley. We remember those good times when the pastures were green and bright. We remember the refreshing cool waters of joy we shared together. We rejoice about the many banquets however lavish or simple they were when we shared good times together. In the midst of all these memories we sense in the background the presence of Jesus. Whether we were aware of it or not, he was there in our midst.

In our sorrow, too, he is with us. His love and presence are always here. He cares for us as a shepherd tenderly cares for the sheep. He cares by watching over them, holding the little lamb that is scared after being lost, singing songs to comfort them in the stormy night. He is here among us today as we grieve. He sits with us, walks with us, cries with us, and laughs with us. He understands our loss but knows that this loss is only temporary for life is eternal and some day we shall be reunited again.

We have gathered today to proclaim the love of our Good Shepherd for NAME and for us who are grieving this day. We have come to celebrate a life that was lived in the presence of our shepherd and of one who was a sign of God's love for us. We celebrate that loving presence of God that was there to greet NAME when she was born on DATE and continued with her throughout her life.

NAME was a somewhat shy person who didn't like to socialize just to socialize, but that doesn't mean she wasn't a people person. She was very friendly and you could usually count on seeing a smile on her face. She took care of her parents everyday with their meals, medications, and doctor visits and she did the same for her mother-in-law. She was liked by the friends of her children and always tried to make the events her children were involved with, even coaching SON's little league team. She obviously loved her family and she said that her husband NAME was the only man she really loved.

Her love for others was also expressed through her volunteering at the hospital and the many notes and postcards she would send to lots of people. She was a fair minded person and always seemed to be able to keep peace in the family which she was very determined should always stay together.

Her loving nature paid dividends as her family grew to be loving people, as well. Everyone was concerned about her when it appeared she should no longer live alone. Knowing that she really wanted to stay in her own home – they struggled with how to make that happen. While all three of the children loved their mother, NAME was the one who moved and came back to take care of her mother for ten years. NAME and NAME are very grateful for that loving sacrifice.

She loved flowers whether it was growing them in her garden or arranging them for display in the house. At the H Lake cabin there was always a bowl of flowers. She was known to send NAME into deep ditches to get her lilies and she always reminded him to look out for snapping turtles. Later it was her grandson, NAME, who got to retrieve cattails for her.

She loved to walk and be out in nature. She would enjoy walks along the river walk and around O Island. She remembered when her husband NAME would play ball for the church team. Although she was not able to attend lately, she always had a very warm spot in her heart for the people of First Church.

Today we commit our loved one into the eternal care of our Good Shepherd knowing that the heavenly fold will be a blessed place for NAME until we see her again. The one who has walked with us and led us throughout our lives will not forsake us at the time of death. Even in the face of death we celebrate that life is eternal. The one who created us out of love receives us back in that love.

We know our loving shepherd will also be with us as we go forth into days of darkness and days of light. We will grieve and we will mourn but we will also hope and cry and laugh. We will find solace in each other and in the presence of the Good Shepherd who is always with us.

The Rainbow
Genesis 9:8-17

Then God said to Noah and to his sons with him, "As for me, I am establishing my covenant with you and your descendants after you, and with every living creature that is with you, the birds, the domestic animals, and every animal of the earth with you, as many as came out of the ark. I establish my covenant with you, that never again shall all flesh be cut off by the waters of a flood, and never again shall there be a flood to destroy the earth."

God said, "This is the sign of the covenant that I make between me and you and every living creature that is with you, for all future generations: I have set my bow in the clouds, and it shall be a sign of the covenant between me and the earth. When I bring clouds over the earth and the bow is seen in the clouds, I will remember my covenant that is between me and you and every living creature of all flesh; and the waters shall never again become a flood to destroy all flesh. When the bow is in the clouds, I will see it and remember the everlasting covenant between God and every living creature of all flesh that is on the earth." God said to Noah, "This is the sign of the covenant that I have established between me and all flesh that is on the earth."

The lesson from Genesis comes after the story of the great flood when Noah and his family have come out of the ark with all the animals. The great flood that God has sent upon earth is now over and God has established the covenant with Noah, his descendants, and all living creatures on earth that there will never again be such a disaster. Never again will God allow the waters of chaos to destroy the earth. As a sign of that covenant God places the rainbow in the sky. Rainbows have become for us a sign of hope and a sign of the presence of God.

There are times in our lives when we really need a sign of hope and a sign that reminds us that God is always with us. We have come to one of those times today as we gather to celebrate the life of *Name* and to mourn our loss at no longer having *him/her* physically present with us. It may seem like the clouds of grief and loss are never ending but we have gathered together today to remind one another that this is not so. We will always miss *Name* and there will be sorrow in the future but there will also be laughter and joy. The rainbows will remind us of this.

The first rainbow is the constant love of our God who does not just walk with us in the sunshine and the happy times but walks with us in the dark and dreary times as well. God is with us at our birth, throughout our lives, and at our death and beyond. Our God is the one who makes the everlasting covenant with us and never fails to keep that promise. Our God is the one who takes death and turns it into resurrection. Our God is the one who comes and weeps with us as we mourn.

We rely on a God who not only leads us into green pastures and by quiet waters but who walks with us in the very darkest places of our lives. Even when we travel through the valley of the shadow of death, we know we

Funeral Sermons that Proclaim and Celebrate

are not alone. This promise is not only for us when we are facing our own death but when we feel its shadow as we grieve for a loved one. God is here as the guiding shepherd to lead us onward and to anoint us with the oil of healing.

Healing will take time and we will still feel the pain of our loss but it will not overwhelm us. Day by day, God will be with us to comfort us and to heal us so that we can deal with our loss. God will be our rainbow today and in the days to come.

The second rainbow is seen in the faces of those who have gathered here today. Not many of us are eloquent in our speech at times like these. They may just give a trite saying or just break down in silence or tears. The eloquence is not in their words but in being here to share this moment. The presence, the hug, the grasp of the hand is a rainbow of hope and love.

We are people of the earth and we often need the physical presence of others. To hear a familiar voice, to see a loved one's face is priceless to us and especially when we are troubled and hurting. Sometimes we just need an angel that is flesh and bones. We are thankful for each one who has reached out and shared in our grief. They are rainbows in the midst of this darkness. And they are also part of God's presence and constant love for us. In each face, the face of God is reflected. In each embrace God wraps us in those loving arms. In every word shared God's voice can be heard as we are reminded that we are cared for and loved.

A third rainbow is in our memories. *Name's* physical presence is no longer with us but *he/she* is with us in all our memories of being together. Let us remember *Name*

Funeral Sermons that Proclaim and Celebrate

and celebrate the ways in which *he/she* continues to be a rainbow for us.

Reflections on the life of the deceased

We will miss the physical presence of *Name* but we know that the joy of this rainbow will continue in the presence of God for all eternity and that someday we will again enjoy the fullness of that blessing. But we do not need to wait until then to celebrate and share that joy *Name* brought into our lives. Whenever we remember *him/her*, whenever we act as a rainbow for others, then *Name* will be with us. And as sure as *he/she* lives on in the presence of God, *he/she* will live on in us in our memories and in our loving deeds.

The Good Shepherd
Psalm 23

The Lord is my shepherd; I shall not want.

He maketh me to lie down in green pastures: he leadeth me beside the still waters.

He restoreth my soul: he leadeth me in the paths of righteousness for his name's sake.

Yea, though I walk through the valley of the shadow of death, I will fear no evil: for thou art with me; thy rod and thy staff they comfort me.

Thou preparest a table before me in the presence of mine enemies: thou anointest my head with oil; my cup runneth over.

Surely goodness and mercy shall follow me all the days of my life: and I will dwell in the house of the Lord forever.

The image of the Good Shepherd is a much beloved one in the church. The idea that God is our shepherd who looks out for us is a reassuring and comforting one. When God is leading us there is nothing that we need besides this. God takes us to green pastures and still waters. God restores and refreshes our souls so that we know peace and joy in our lives. No matter what happens, however bad it seems, we know that God is with us to comfort us and guide us. God is generous to supply our needs and blesses us forever more. Our greatest joy is to be with God.

It is no wonder that the church took up that image with Jesus and it has become a large part of how we understand him. He is the one who leads us and watches over us. He seeks us when we are lost and he carries us in his arms of love. He is the one who leads us by the still waters where we refresh ourselves during the dry times of life. He is the one who leads us to green pastures where we are fed and strengthened for our journey. He is the one who restores our souls when life tries to tear us apart. He is the one who sets the table of banquet where we rejoice in the goodness of life and celebrate the love that surrounds us.

Each Sunday morning as we gather for worship, we celebrate the presence of the risen Christ who comes to be our Good Shepherd. In the reading of the scriptures, the hymns, prayers, sermons, sacraments, and the fellowship before or afterwards, Christ is present to us. We find ourselves being refreshed and renewed for our daily lives as we spend time together in the presence of our shepherd.

He is, also, the one who walks with us through the dark valleys, even the valley of death. Today we look for the comfort in a time of darkness and loss. It is sometimes difficult to sense him in the darkness but if we listen carefully we will hear his voice of guidance and care. Sometimes that voice comes through others who speak to us. It is sometimes easier to hear the divine voice when we hear it through human words. Sometimes that love is most evident to us when we can see it in action through flesh and blood.

Today we gather to share our love and our stories with one another. We come to hear the voice of the Good

Funeral Sermons that Proclaim and Celebrate

Shepherd reflected in the voices of family and friends. We cry together, we laugh together, and we know that in both we are embraced in the arms of our loving God. Today we share more than the time in the dark valley. We remember those good times when the pastures were green and bright. We remember the refreshing cool waters of joy we shared together. We rejoice about the many banquets however lavish or simple they were when we shared good times together. In the midst of all these memories we sense in the background the presence of Jesus. Whether we were aware of it or not, he was there in our midst.

In our sorrow, too, he is with us. His love and presence are always here. He cares for us as a shepherd tenderly cares for the sheep. He is watching over them, holding the little lamb that is scared after being lost, singing songs to comfort them in the stormy night. He is here among us today as we grieve. He sits with us, walks with us, cries with us, and laughs with us. He understands our loss but knows that this loss is only temporary for life is eternal and some day we shall be reunited again.

We have gathered today to proclaim the love of our Good Shepherd for *Name* and for us who are grieving this day. We have come to celebrate a life that was lived in the presence of our shepherd and of one who was a sign of God's love for us. We celebrate that loving presence of God that was there to greet *Name* when *he/she* was born....

Personal reflection

Today we commit our loved one into the eternal care of our Good Shepherd knowing that the heavenly fold will be a blessed place for *Name* until we see *him/her* again.

Funeral Sermons that Proclaim and Celebrate

The one who has walked with us and lead us throughout our lives will not forsake us at the time of death. Even in the face of death we celebrate that life is eternal. The one who created us out of love receives us back in that love.

We know our loving shepherd will also be with us as we go forth into days of darkness and days of light. We will grieve and we will mourn but we will also hope and cry and laugh. We will find solace in each other and in the presence of the Good Shepherd who is always with us.

A Time

Ecclesiastes 3:1-15

For everything there is a season, and a time for every matter under heaven: a time to be born, and a time to die; a time to plant, and a time to pluck up what is planted; a time to kill, and a time to heal; a time to break down, and a time to build up; a time to weep, and a time to laugh; a time to mourn, and a time to dance; a time to throw away stones, and a time to gather stones together; a time to embrace, and a time to refrain from embracing; a time to seek, and a time to lose; a time to keep, and a time to throw away; a time to tear, and a time to sew; a time to keep silence, and a time to speak; a time to love, and a time to hate; a time for war, and a time for peace. What gain have the workers from their toil? I have seen the business that God has given to everyone to be busy with.

He has made everything suitable for its time; moreover he has put a sense of past and future into their minds, yet they cannot find out what God has done from the beginning to the end. I know that there is nothing better for them than to be happy and enjoy themselves as long as they live; moreover, it is God's gift that all should eat and drink and take pleasure in all their toil. I know that whatever God does endures forever; nothing can be added to it, nor anything taken from it; God has done this, so that all should stand in awe before him. That which is, already has been; that which is to be, already is; and God seeks out what has gone by.

Funeral Sermons that Proclaim and Celebrate

We are creatures of time. We mark it with clocks and calendars plus we celebrate special seasons and times. We remember birthdays and anniversaries - and we remember losses and deaths. We set aside special times in our lives such as infancy, childhood, and adulthood. Things that are appropriate in one time are not deemed appropriate in others. You can suck your thumb when you are six months of age but unless you just hit your thumb with a hammer people expect that you won't do that when you are thirty years old. We spend a portion of our years learning, then working and then retiring.

The preacher or teacher who is the unnamed author of these words we heard today from Ecclesiastes lines out some of the things that have been given their times. There is a time to plant and a time to reap. There is a time to keep and a time to throw away. There is a time to rend and a time to sew. There is a time to be born and a time to die. And as we are experiencing today there is a time to mourn. But we must also remember that there is a time to dance. There is a time to weep but also a time to laugh.

We have been granted a wondrous gift in our ability to understand time and to remember. We can imagine things that are to come and we can summon the past and relive it in our minds. This is part of God's gift to us as children of God. It is also God's gift for us to eat, drink and take pleasure in our work here on earth. God is not a hard task master who demands stern faces and serious looks all the time. God loves us and desires us to enjoy this wonderful creation which has been given to us.

So today is a time of remembering. It is a time to mourn and cry but it is also a time to laugh. God understands our

Funeral Sermons that Proclaim and Celebrate

time of mourning but it is not meant to last forever. Our memory of *Name* will continue as long as we are alive and there will always be a soft, somewhat painful place in our hearts for *him/her*. But there is also a time of healing. Part of that healing is in remembering the good things about *Name*. We remember that *he/she*....

Personal reflections

Our time of mourning will not end with the service but our time of healing is already here. We have celebrated the life of *Name* and we have recalled the love and care our God has for *him/her* and for us. So we will trust our loved one into God's eternal presence and we will look forward to that time in the future when we will laugh and dance with *him/her*.

Come To The Feast
Isaiah 25:6-9

On this mountain the Lord of hosts will make for all peoples a feast of rich food, a feast of well-aged wines, of rich food filled with marrow, of well-aged wines strained clear. And he will destroy on this mountain the shroud that is cast over all peoples, the sheet that is spread over all nations; he will swallow up death forever. Then the Lord God will wipe away the tears from all faces, and the disgrace of his people he will take away from all the earth, for the Lord has spoken.

It will be said on that day, Lo, this is our God; we have waited for him, so that he might save us. This is the Lord for whom we have waited; let us be glad and rejoice in his salvation.

Most of us really look forward to special meals. Thanksgiving is probably the biggest feast day for us with Christmas and Easter close behind. While we enjoy any good meal there is something really special about a feast. It doesn't even have to be a huge meal just as long as it is special. A couple of really good cheeses with fresh fruit can make for a feast especially when shared with someone that means a great deal to us. Isaiah taps into this part of our humanity when he describes God's desire for us. God is going to throw a banquet for us. It will be a feast with

Funeral Sermons that Proclaim and Celebrate

rich, delicious food and wondrous wines. It will be the kind of feast that most of his audience could only dream about probably. It will be a feast that they couldn't prepare for themselves.

This feast goes well beyond the planned menu, though. For at this feast God is going to remove all that shrouds and clouds our lives. The tears from our faces will be wiped away and mourning will be destroyed. All that holds us back from living as children of God will be taken away and we will feast with light hearts in the presence of our God. This is what God desires for us. This is the love that God offers us each and every day.

Today we are all too aware of what it means to cry and to mourn and yet underneath all that is: the sense that God is with us and desires to heal our hurts. We have come together today to mourn the loss of our loved one, *Name*. In the past few days we have known crying and mourning as we prepared for this service, this time of saying goodbye. And yet it is with the hope that we are also saying that we will see *him/her* later. This is not a final goodbye but a parting for a time. We look forward to that wonderful banquet that God has in store for us when in the presence of God, we will be reunited with all our loved ones.

It will be a celebration beyond comparison and I imagine that we will gather around those tables and remember good times. So, we will be rehearsing today for that time. *If there is a meal after the service that connection can be made here.* Let us celebrate the life *Name* lived among us anticipating the day we will again share with *him/her* at that heavenly banquet.

Funeral Sermons that Proclaim and Celebrate

Name was....

Personal reflections

It has been good for us to reflect on a life well lived, a person who loved and was loved. So know we commend *Name* into the presence of God where *he/she* will dwell until we gather with *him/her* at that banquet table and celebrate the love that God has allowed us to share.

Comfort My People
Isaiah 40:1-8

Comfort, O comfort my people, says your God. Speak tenderly to Jerusalem, and cry to her that she has served her term, that her penalty is paid, that she has received from the Lord's hand double for all her sins.

A voice cries out: "In the wilderness prepare the way of the Lord, make straight in the desert a highway for our God. Every valley shall be lifted up, and every mountain and hill be made low; the uneven ground shall become level, and the rough places a plain. Then the glory of the Lord shall be revealed, and all people shall see it together, for the mouth of the Lord has spoken." A voice says, "Cry out!" And I said, "What shall I cry?" All people are grass, their constancy is like the flower of the field. The grass withers, the flower fades, when the breath of the Lord blows upon it; surely the people are grass. The grass withers, the flower fades; but the word of our God will stand forever.

Life sometimes just doesn't seem fair. We wonder sometimes if the whole world has turned against us and, sometimes, we even wonder whose side God is on. It must have been that way for the people of Israel who were in exile. Uprooted from their homes and families they were brought to a strange land. Rumors of the temple and the

Funeral Sermons that Proclaim and Celebrate

walls of Jerusalem being destroyed had passed through their midst. They have been in exile so long that these are all second or third generation folks who only know the splendor David's kingdom from stories.

Suffering comes from many sources. Sometimes it is the direct consequence of poor decisions that we ourselves have made. We allow our anger to get the best of us and we quit our job when we have no prospects for another one. We disregard all the advice of health professionals and continue practices that put our health and even our lives at risk. We choose to look out only for ourselves and soon those we loved have been pushed out of our lives.

Sometimes we are just at the end of a chain of consequences that we had nothing to do about. Like the people who were born in exile, we find ourselves living in a toxic world that destroys our health because of the actions and inactions of those who went before us. Sometimes it just seems like bad luck. We were at the wrong place at the wrong time and ended up in an accident. We have taken good care of our bodies, but we still find ourselves with a terrible disease. Sometimes life just isn't fair.

It seems that way today as we mourn the loss of *Name*. (Verbalize for the congregation why this death seems so unfair to us.)

And yet in the midst of all, this the word comes from God that comfort is on the horizon. Right now it sounds unbelievable that we will ever find comfort. We are in pain and grief and sorrow. We are in shock and half numb. The idea of finding comfort seems so very far away. Just as those in exile must have found the thought of comfort to be incredible and unreachable, so we feel the loss in our

Funeral Sermons that Proclaim and Celebrate

lives. And yet, that word of God comes that comfort is on the way. Our pain will not be forever. Our grief will be lifted from our shoulders. We will find healing and wholeness and hope.

As distant as comfort seems today, the testimony of the people of God is that this word can be trusted. The God who created us, loved us and redeemed us is faithful to bring us healing and wholeness. It seldom comes in one moment. It is more likely to come over a period of time, sometimes years, but it comes. The Spirit of God hovers over us and covers us with wings of love and care. The Good Shepherd walks with us in the darkest of places and times. As Jesus wept with Mary and Martha at the tomb of Lazarus, so he weeps with us today. He weeps with us because he knows our grief and loss and because we are deeply loved by God.

The healing and comfort will come through family and friends who share our pain like these who are gathered with us today. The kind words, the hugs, the casserole dishes are all signs of the love of God that is being spread by these folks. The healing will come in memories which will remind us of the love that was shared with *Name*. As you have gathered as family and friends you have been sharing some of these memories and beginning to sow those seeds of healing. We continue that process today as remember *Name* and the way God's love was shared with us through *his/her* life.

Personal reflections

"Comfort, O comfort my people.... Speak tenderly...." God comes to speak tenderly to us today. We remember

Funeral Sermons that Proclaim and Celebrate

Name today and celebrate their life. We reach out to one another to offer comfort. And we trust that as God now receives *Name* into the depths of God's love for all eternity, so God wraps us in that love, as well.

Hope In The Midst Of Despair
Isaiah 40:28-31

Have you not known? Have you not heard? The Lord is the everlasting God, the creator of the ends of the earth. He does not faint or grow weary; his understanding is unsearchable. He gives power to the faint, and strengthens the powerless. Even youths will faint and be weary, and the young will fall exhausted; but those who wait for the Lord shall renew their strength, they shall mount up with wings like eagles, they shall run and not be weary, they shall walk and not faint.

Psalm 23

The Lord is my shepherd; I shall not want.

He maketh me to lie down in green pastures: he leadeth me beside the still waters.

He restoreth my soul: he leadeth me in the paths of righteousness for his name's sake.

Yea, though I walk through the valley of the shadow of death, I will fear no evil: for thou art with me; thy rod and thy staff they comfort me.

Thou preparest a table before me in the presence of mine enemies: thou anointest my head with oil; my cup runneth over.

Surely goodness and mercy shall follow me all the days of my life: and I will dwell in the house of the Lord forever.

Funeral Sermons that Proclaim and Celebrate

Revelation 21:1-7

Then I saw a new heaven and a new earth; for the first heaven and the first earth had passed away, and the sea was no more. And I saw the holy city, the new Jerusalem, coming down out of heaven from God, prepared as a bride adorned for her husband. And I heard a loud voice from the throne saying, "See, the home of God is among mortals. He will dwell with them as their God; they will be his peoples, and God himself will be with them; he will wipe every tear from their eyes. Death will be no more; mourning and crying and pain will be no more, for the first things have passed away." And the one who was seated on the throne said, "See, I am making all things new." Also he said, "Write this, for these words are trustworthy and true." Then he said to me, "It is done! I am the Alpha and the Omega, the beginning and the end. To the thirsty I will give water as a gift from the spring of the water of life. Those who conquer will inherit these things, and I will be their God and they will be my children.

John 14:1-4, 18-19, 25-27

"Do not let your hearts be troubled. Believe in God, believe also in me. In my Father's house there are many dwelling places. If it were not so, would I have told you that I go to prepare a place for you? And if I go and prepare a place for you, I will come again and will take you to myself, so that where I am, there you may be also.

And you know the way to the place where I am going."

"I will not leave you orphaned; I am coming to you. In a little while the world will no longer see me, but you will see me; because I live, you also will live.

"I have said these things to you while I am still with you.

Funeral Sermons that Proclaim and Celebrate

But the Advocate, the Holy Spirit, whom the Father will send in my name, will teach you everything, and remind you of all that I have said to you. Peace I leave with you; my peace I give to you. I do not give to you as the world gives. Do not let your hearts be troubled, and do not let them be afraid.

N.B. This sermon is based on the four scripture readings. One may read all four during the service which is often my practice, or one may use just portions of the scriptures added into the appropriate paragraphs or one may simply omit one or more of the paragraphs as each of the first four paragraphs are linked to the readings in the order above.

The words of the prophet Isaiah sound so lofty and serene: "Those who wait upon the Lord shall renew their strength, they shall mount up with wings like eagles." Yet we know that Isaiah spoke those words from God to a nation that had been defeated and was now in exile; separated from everything they knew and loved. Many of them must have thought that things would never get better. They probably felt like giving up. And yet even in these darkest of times, God sent a word of hope.

The beautiful words of the twenty-third Psalm tell us of a wonderful peace where we can feel watched over and cared for by the shepherd. It talks of abundance and of confidence. And yet these words come to us from David's experience of walking through the valley of deep darkness. He knew what it was like to face his own sin. He knew what it was like to lose loved ones, his own children, to death. David gave us these words not because his life was easy but because he had faced that dark valley and found God was there with him. When we are facing the times of our deepest darkness, God does not leave us alone but stands beside us and weeps with us and then speaks words of hope to us.

We often turn to the wonderful imagery of the book of Revelation with its promise of no more tears and no more sorrow. We love the image of God dwelling among us and of us being God's people. We are comforted by the idea of there being no more death. These are words of hope and faith that strengthen us. But, again, John did not have these visions because he was experiencing that everything was good and right. He was in exile on Patmos. It looked from every human standpoint that Rome would win and the church would be destroyed. But in the midst of that horrible reality, he saw God's promise that things would be better. God and life would win. The promise of Revelation is that no matter how difficult life seems we will come through this as we trust in God.

In the gospel of John, we have those words of Jesus as he promises that in God's world there are plenty of homes and that Jesus will come and take us to himself that we may always dwell with our God. He invites us to give up our fears and to not let our hearts be troubled. Jesus gives us these promises even as he knows he is facing his own arrest, crucifixion, and death. The love of Jesus is so strong for us that even in the face of his own execution, he gives us words of comfort. He spoke them to those first disciples and he speaks them again to us.

If we will seek God's strength we will find that we can fly like an eagle; if we will but put out our hand we will

Funeral Sermons that Proclaim and Celebrate

find the Good Shepherd walking beside us. If we will but open our hearts, we will find that God is offering us the peace that the world cannot take away. If we will listen, we will hear the voice of Jesus speaking peace and grace to us.

We gather today in a time of deep darkness as we mourn the loss of *Name*. Yet even as we are aware of the pain of separation and the distress of losing the physical presence of *Name*, we are aware of the presence of God who comes to comfort us and to assure us of the eternal nature of life. We know the comfort of a God who declares to us that Jesus has died our death and has been raised for our sake, so that as he now lives eternally with God so we also shall live eternally. We know the comfort of a God who has created us with memories, so that we can remember with fondness the life of *Name*. But it is more than just remembering *him/her* for *he/she* still lives in and through those who knew *him/her*.

You all have your special memories of *Name*. It might be *personal reflections*.... These memories will always be a precious part of your lives. But we rejoice not only in the memories of *his/her* life but in the ways that *he/she* still lives in and through all who knew *him/her*. In every act of kindness and love that is accomplished by those who knew *him/her*, *Name* will still be there. May *his/her* memory be ever blessed and *his/her* loving and caring spirit live forever in you.

Come And Rest
Matthew 5:3-10

"Blessed are the poor in spirit, for theirs is the kingdom of heaven. "Blessed are those who mourn, for they will be comforted. "Blessed are the meek, for they will inherit the earth. "Blessed are those who hunger and thirst for righteousness, for they will be filled. "Blessed are the merciful, for they will receive mercy. "Blessed are the pure in heart, for they will see God. "Blessed are the peacemakers, for they will be called children of God. "Blessed are those who are persecuted for righteousness' sake, for theirs is the kingdom of heaven."

Matthew 11:28-30

"Come to me, all you that are weary and are carrying heavy burdens, and I will give you rest. Take my yoke upon you, and learn from me; for I am gentle and humble in heart, and you will find rest for your souls. For my yoke is easy, and my burden is light."

We all have had times when we were just exhausted. Maybe it was a day of really hard, physical labor or a night of restless anxiety. Whether physical or mental we understand what it is to be weary, worn out, done in. It seems like we have carried a heavy burden that only grows heavier the farther we tote it. It drains our energy,

Funeral Sermons that Proclaim and Celebrate

our spirit, and our joy.

And, hopefully, we have all had those times when we were relieved of our burden and offered respite and refreshment. To come home at the end of a hard day to sit in a comfortable chair with a refreshing drink and a loved one to share the day with is a joy. When we have fretted through the night and then in the morning we have found that our worst fears were not realized and that things are going to be alright is a lifting of a burden of the soul. We all long for those moments.

Jesus understood the burdens and labors of the folk he encountered as he taught and he understands our burdens and labors, as well. He not only understands, but he offers to take our burdens from us and welcome us into a time of rest. He takes our heavy burden and offers one that is light as we yoke ourselves up with him. When we walk together with Jesus in God's realm, we find our burdens are light and our days and nights are restful.

The Beatitudes, those 'blessed are they....' sayings that open what we call the Sermon on the Mount, are a snapshot of what it means to walk with Jesus. In God's realm things are different from this world. The advice is not to do unto others before they have a chance to do unto you. Nor is it to take all you can whenever you can. Nor is it to always look out for number one. In God's world we are called to be humble, meek, seek peace and righteousness. We are called to be merciful and pure in our heart. When we find ourselves mourning, we are called to accept that. There is a beautiful passage from on old Jewish prayer book, "Though the longing within us seems more than we can bear, we know that our grief is according to our blessing.

Funeral Sermons that Proclaim and Celebrate

The sorrow of separation is the inevitable price of days and years of precious love; tears are the tender tribute of yearning affection for those who have passed away but cannot be forgotten." Mourning is not something to avoid but to accept as the price of having someone to love.

As we enter into our grief, shed our tears, and remember the life of our loved ones, we begin to find comfort. It doesn't take away our sadness and make everything all bright and shiny in a moment but it does begin the healing process. As we come to terms with the fact that our sadness is because we have been blessed and as we recount the blessings we received from knowing and loving someone, comfort comes.

So today we have gathered to mourn together. We have gathered to cry together and to remember the life of *Name*. *His/Her* life has been a blessing to those of us gathered here. As you remember *Name* in your heart let us reflect on those blessings.

Personal reflections

Name was a person who....

As God calls *Name* into that place of eternal rest where the burdens of life are over, may our memories and reflections bring us comfort in the days and months to come.

Jesus Walks With Us
Luke 24:13-35

Now on that same day two of them were going to a village called Emmaus, about seven miles from Jerusalem, and talking with each other about all these things that had happened. While they were talking and discussing, Jesus himself came near and went with them, but their eyes were kept from recognizing him. And he said to them, "What are you discussing with each other while you walk along?" They stood still, looking sad. Then one of them, whose name was Cleopas, answered him, "Are you the only stranger in Jerusalem who does not know the things that have taken place there in these days?" He asked them, "What things?" They replied, "The things about Jesus of Nazareth, who was a prophet mighty in deed and word before God and all the people, and how our chief priests and leaders handed him over to be condemned to death and crucified him. But we had hoped that he was the one to redeem Israel. Yes, and besides all this, it is now the third day since these things took place. Moreover, some women of our group astounded us. They were at the tomb early this morning, and when they did not find his body there, they came back and told us that they had indeed seen a vision of angels who said that he was alive. Some of those who were with us went to the tomb and found it just as the women had said; but they did not see him." Then he said to them, "Oh, how foolish you are, and how slow of heart to believe all that the prophets have declared! Was it not necessary that the Messiah should suffer these things and then enter into his glory?" Then beginning with Moses and all the prophets, he interpreted to them the things about himself in all the scriptures. As they came near the village to which they were going, he walked ahead as if he were going on. But they urged him strongly, saying, "Stay with us, because it is almost evening and the day is now nearly over." So he went in to stay with them. When he was at the table with them, he took bread, blessed and broke it, and gave it to them. Then their eyes were opened, and they recognized him; and he vanished from their sight. They said to each other, "Were not our hearts burning within us while he was talking to us on the road, while he was opening the scriptures to us?" That same hour they got up and returned to Jerusalem; and they found the eleven and their companions gathered together. They were saying, "The Lord has risen indeed, and he has appeared to Simon!" Then they told what had happened on the road, and how he had been made known to them in the breaking of the bread.

The story from the gospel of Luke is a familiar one which we often refer to as the Walk to Emmaus. Two of Jesus' disciples who are not part of the twelve are going from Jerusalem back to their homes in Emmaus. They are heartbroken for Jesus has been crucified. The one they counted on had been lost and they were in grief and despair. Someone came along beside them as they were walking and inquired why they were so sad. The two were incredulous. How could anyone not know of their loss? Jesus asked them to tell him about what happened. He

Funeral Sermons that Proclaim and Celebrate

listened for a while and then began to share with them the scriptures. He explained the way of God's love and then in a final act when they reached Emmaus, he broke bread with them and they realized who he was. He disappeared but they, in their joy, ran back to Jerusalem to share the good news.

Sounds pretty familiar doesn't it? Not only that we have heard the story before but because it sounds a lot like what we have experienced. One whom we loved and on whom we counted is gone from our midst. We are in grief and on the brink of despair. We feel like our world has been torn apart and we see no way for it to be put back together again. So we have gathered here today to tell our stories. We have come to share what *Name* has meant to us. We have come to hear from scripture and to hear some explanation of where God's love is in the midst of all of this. Perhaps at some time, if not today then later in our grieving, our eyes may be opened and we might catch a glimpse of Jesus who is here with us. He has come to share our sorrow, to walk with us in our grief, and to hold is in the tender love of our God.

So let us remember *Name* and know that we are sharing these memories not only with each other but with the one who loves us more than we can know. *Name* was ....

Personal Reflections

Jesus is here among us and will continue to be with us as we go through our days and months ahead. We can talk with him at any time and share our memories and our grief. As we turn to the scriptures we can listen for his voice and we can anticipate his caring embrace. For while

Funeral Sermons that Proclaim and Celebrate

our grief is deep and real we know that death is not the final word. Jesus comes and reminds us that love and life are the end that God has for all of us.

Many Rooms
John 14:1-14, 18-19, 25-27

"Do not let your hearts be troubled. Believe in God, believe also in me. In my Father's house there are many dwelling places. If it were not so, would I have told you that I go to prepare a place for you? And if I go and prepare a place for you, I will come again and will take you to myself, so that where I am, there you may be also.

And you know the way to the place where I am going." Thomas said to him, "Lord, we do not know where you are going. How can we know the way?" Jesus said to him, "I am the way, and the truth, and the life. No one comes to the Father except through me. If you know me, you will know my Father also. From now on you do know him and have seen him." Philip said to him, "Lord, show us the Father, and we will be satisfied." Jesus said to him, "Have I been with you all this time, Philip, and you still do not know me? Whoever has seen me has seen the Father. How can you say, 'Show us the Father'? Do you not believe that I am in the Father and the Father is in me? The words that I say to you I do not speak on my own; but the Father who dwells in me does his works. Believe me that I am in the Father and the Father is in me; but if you do not, then believe me because of the works themselves.

Very truly, I tell you, the one who believes in me will also do the works that I do and, in fact, will do greater works than these,

Funeral Sermons that Proclaim and Celebrate

because I am going to the Father. I will do whatever you ask in my name, so that the Father may be glorified in the Son. If in my name you ask me for anything, I will do it.

"I will not leave you orphaned; I am coming to you. In a little while the world will no longer see me, but you will see me; because I live, you also will live.

"I have said these things to you while I am still with you. But the Advocate, the Holy Spirit, whom the Father will send in my name, will teach you everything, and remind you of all that I have said to you. Peace I leave with you; my peace I give to you. I do not give to you as the world gives. Do not let your hearts be troubled, and do not let them be afraid.

It must have been a somber time when Jesus gathered his disciples around him for what would be their last meal together. The events of the week were dramatic and scary. When Jesus entered into Jerusalem and was greeted with the enthusiastic crowd it would have been very exciting. But with the Romans in charge it was also very dangerous. The Romans did not tolerate anything that looked like rebellion and the consequences were meted out quickly and severely. The usual punishment was crucifixion. Jesus and his disciples were on the Romans' radar, so to speak.

In the midst of all this tension, Jesus gathered his disciples for a time of celebrating, teaching and fellowship. Yet the dark mood continues as Jesus reveals that for him the end is near and that one his twelve closest disciples will betray him. He has told the disciples that he is going away and that they cannot go with him at this time. It is a time of sadness and grief. It is a time of separation and sorrow. It is not unlike our time today. We have gathered to care for

Funeral Sermons that Proclaim and Celebrate

and support one another in our time of grieving. We feel the separation that death brings and we are looking for a word of comfort.

Jesus had compassion on his disciples that day and he has compassion on us today. The words he spoke to John and Peter and the rest he now speaks to us. "Do not let your hearts be troubled." Oh, how our troubled hearts yearn to be comforted. We seek some word of consolation but how can we still our troubled hearts? Jesus says, "Believe in God, believe also in me." Ah, there is our answer, the source of our comfort. We look beyond the human and the earthly and turn our attention to God, the eternal one. We focus on the one who created life and who is life eternal and on Jesus who brought that life to us and our world.

For Jesus reminds us that in God's realm there is plenty of room. There are plenty of dwelling places for us with God and Jesus is preparing them for us. He knows us and knows what we need to feel at home in God's house. And not only will Jesus prepare the place for us but Jesus will join us there. Where he is going, we are also going. To a place where there is no more separation, no more grief, and no more tears. We are going to a place prepared for us by the one who loves us eternally.

What do you suppose Jesus has prepared for *Name?* Given what we know about *Name,* we can make some educated guesses.

Personal reflections

(There will be a fishing pole because they liked to fish. Season tickets to State U football games. Loved ones who have gone before.)

Funeral Sermons that Proclaim and Celebrate

We are sad this day and we are missing the physical presence of our loved one but we know that Jesus is there with them to assure them of God's love for them and to welcome them into God's house. We will mourn and we will cry for a time but we do so with hope for we know that there is a place being prepared for us with our loved ones.

If God Is For Us
Romans 8:31-39

What then are we to say about these things? If God is for us, who is against us? He who did not withhold his own Son, but gave him up for all of us, will he not with him also give us everything else? Who will bring any charge against God's elect? It is God who justifies. Who is to condemn? It is Christ Jesus, who died, yes, who was raised, who is at the right hand of God, who indeed intercedes for us. Who will separate us from the love of Christ? Will hardship, or distress, or persecution, or famine, or nakedness, or peril, or sword? As it is written, "For your sake we are being killed all day long; we are accounted as sheep to be slaughtered." No, in all these things we are more than conquerors through him who loved us. For I am convinced that neither death, nor life, nor angels, nor rulers, nor things present, nor things to come, nor powers, nor height, nor depth, nor anything else in all creation, will be able to separate us from the love of God in Christ Jesus our Lord.

"If God is for us, who can be against us?" What a strange and yet delightful question! The answer is so obvious to us we wonder why it would even be asked. And yet all of us know that sometimes we need to be reminded of the most obvious of things. The answer, of course, is no one and nothing can stand against us if God is for us. And God is for us. God is the one who did not withhold the only begotten but gave him for us and for our salvation. The one who has given us the most precious gift imaginable is definitely for us.

This great love of God for us has been shown in the life, death, and resurrection of Christ Jesus. He has lived among us to teach us how much we are loved by God and how we can live into wholeness and healing as part of God's reign here on earth. He died so that we might know the depth of God's love and he was raised so that we might know the power of God. This Jesus who is our salvation now sits enthroned at the right hand of God interceding for us, praying for us.

We are indeed beloved of God. We experience that love in many ways and one of those was in the life that *Name* lived among us. Through *his/her* life we have been blessed with the presence of God among us.

Personal reflections on the blessing the deceased brought

With all of this love directed to us by our powerful, life giving God it is no wonder that we are reminded that nothing can separate us from the love of God in Christ Jesus. Life cannot separate us from God's love and neither can death. While death is a painful time of separation for us as the physical presence of our loved one is no longer with us, we know that they are now in the full presence of God's love. We ache with longing because we desire to be with our loved one as we use to be and that is no longer possible. But the love we shared with them is still

Funeral Sermons that Proclaim and Celebrate

alive and active. That cannot be broken for it is part of that eternal love of God which holds all of God's children.

Nothing in all of creation can separate us from the love of God and that includes our sorrow and grief. As we reflect on the love of God that refuses to be defeated by anything, as we allow the reality of the love to hold us and comfort us in our sorrow, we can begin to allow that love to heal us. We will always remember *Name* and we will always miss *him/her*. But our grief is based on love and it will be healed with love.

Throughout the days, weeks, and, yes, years ahead allow the good memories of the love that *Name* shared with you comfort you and heal you. For our beloved is not really gone from us. They are as close as the love of God which wraps us in loving arms.

Love
I Corinthians 13

If I speak in the tongues of mortals and of angels, but do not have love, I am a noisy gong or a clanging cymbal. And if I have prophetic powers, and understand all mysteries and all knowledge, and if I have all faith, so as to remove mountains, but do not have love, I am nothing. If I give away all my possessions, and if I hand over my body so that I may boast, but do not have love, I gain nothing.

Love is patient; love is kind; love is not envious or boastful or arrogant or rude. It does not insist on its own way; it is not irritable or resentful; it does not rejoice in wrongdoing, but rejoices in the truth. It bears all things, believes all things, hopes all things, endures all things.

Love never ends. But as for prophecies, they will come to an end; as for tongues, they will cease; as for knowledge, it will come to an end. For we know only in part, and we prophesy only in part; but when the complete comes, the partial will come to an end. When I was a child, I spoke like a child, I thought like a child, I reasoned like a child; when I became an adult, I put an end to childish ways. For now we see in a mirror, dimly, but then we will see face to face. Now I know only in part; then I will know fully, even as I have been fully known. And now faith, hope, and love abide, these three; and the greatest of these is love.

Funeral Sermons that Proclaim and Celebrate

The love chapter, as the thirteenth chapter of 1 Corinthians is often called, is often read at weddings rather than at a funeral but we have shared that scripture today because it reflects so well the life of *Name*. The sharing of love was not an afterthought for *her/him* but was at the very center of their being.

Name had a great love for *her/his* family.

Personal reflections on the family life

Having shared so much love within the family that love was not exhausted but, instead, grew and reached out to others. *Reflections on how Name shared love beyond family. You may then include things that they loved doing, as well.*

We want to celebrate today that life of love but we need to do more than that for we need to continue it. For when we are patient and kind we will not only be honoring the memory of *Name* but we will be sharing *her/his* love and spirit with others. When we refrain from being envious or boastful, arrogant or rude then *Name* will live on in and through us. When we allow others to have their say rather than insisting on our being in charge, then the life of *Name* goes forth again in our actions.

When we strive to be pleasant in unpleasant circumstance; when we do not take offense when offense has been given then the great love of God which was so evident in *Name's* life will be evident once again. When we refrain from taking delight in what is wrong but instead insist that the just and merciful way be taken then we lift up the life of *Name*.

It is good for us to come together today to support and care for one another and to celebrate the loving life

Funeral Sermons that Proclaim and Celebrate

Name shared with us. But in the days and years ahead we will bring even more honor to *her/him* as we bear the unbearable, believe in the unbelievable, hope in the midst of despair, and as we endure to the end. May today not mark the end of *Name's* life but only a time of transition so that as *she/he* lives on eternally with God, *she/he* may continue to live in and through each of us.

God's Fullness Within Us
Ephesians 3:14-21

For this reason I bow my knees before the Father, from whom every family in heaven and on earth takes its name. I pray that, according to the riches of his glory, he may grant that you may be strengthened in your inner being with power through his Spirit, and that Christ may dwell in your hearts through faith, as you are being rooted and grounded in love. I pray that you may have the power to comprehend, with all the saints, what is the breadth and length and height and depth, and to know the love of Christ that surpasses knowledge, so that you may be filled with all the fullness of God. Now to him who by the power at work within us is able to accomplish abundantly far more than all we can ask or imagine, to him be glory in the church and in Christ Jesus to all generations, forever and ever. Amen.

Paul has a prayer for the people of Ephesus and he knows that his prayer is based on substantial resources. He prays out of the riches of the glory of God for the Ephesian Christians. He bases his prayer not just on his good wishes or his ability to make a difference in their lives but on the riches of God's glory. And his prayer is direct. He is praying for these folks to be strengthened in their inner beings with power through the Spirit. That strength

Funeral Sermons that Proclaim and Celebrate

will allow Christ to dwell in their hearts and to ground them in love. It is a wonderful prayer for the church at Ephesus but it is not just for them. This letter is included in our scriptures because it contains the power of God that reaches far beyond the time and place of Paul's writing of it. It extends throughout time and space to us. It is Paul's prayer for us and our prayer for each other this day.

At the time of death there are often questions we ask. *Why this person? Why now? Why did they die in this way?* Sometimes we even ask, *Where is God?* These are normal questions and we should not feel that we are unfaithful to God because we ask them. We are hurting and dealing with great loss in our lives. It is okay to have questions. It is okay to address them to God. It is okay because as we open up our hearts to God in our grief, we open up our hearts to God's love.

That is the result of our being strengthened in the power of God's Spirit. This is the result of our allowing Christ to dwell in our hearts. We begin to comprehend that which is incomprehensible: the depth and breadth and length and height of God's love for us. It is a love so incredible and strong that we will never be able to understand it in its fullness. It is a love that is constant and pure. It is a love that never ends. It is a love that cannot be broken by death or by grief. It is the love that fills us with the fullness of God, who is love.

We have experienced that love of God in our lives. We have experienced it in the life of *Name*. *He/she* has lived among us and shared *his/her* life with us and in doing so has shared the love and life of God with us. We remember and celebrate that life today.

Funeral Sermons that Proclaim and Celebrate

God's love came to us through *Name*....

Personal reflections

And now we release *Name* into that great love of God and we offer ourselves into that love, as well. It is the love that will hold us and bind up our wounds. It is the love that will help our hearts to heal. And they will heal. It will take time and it will not always be easy. And the hurt will not go away completely. We will always have a tender spot in our hearts for *Name* and for what *he/she* meant to us. But as God's healing Spirit works in our hearts our wounds will become like the wounds of the Christ. They did not go away but they became glorious. Over time, with the healing love of God expressed by God's people and God's Spirit our wounds will became glorious memories of one we love even though *he/she* is no longer physically among us. *Name* now resides completely in the fullness of God and as that fullness is growing within us, so *he/she* will always be with us.

And The Sea Was No More
Revelation 21:1-7

Then I saw a new heaven and a new earth; for the first heaven and the first earth had passed away, and the sea was no more. And I saw the holy city, the new Jerusalem, coming down out of heaven from God, prepared as a bride adorned for her husband. And I heard a loud voice from the throne saying, "See, the home of God is among mortals. He will dwell with them as their God; they will be his peoples, and God himself will be with them; he will wipe every tear from their eyes. Death will be no more; mourning and crying and pain will be no more, for the first things have passed away." And the one who was seated on the throne said, "See, I am making all things new." Also he said, "Write this, for these words are trustworthy and true." Then he said to me, "It is done! I am the Alpha and the Omega, the beginning and the end. To the thirsty I will give water as a gift from the spring of the water of life. Those who conquer will inherit these things, and I will be their God and they will be my children.

In the beginning when God began to create, God hovered over the waters of chaos. God placed the dome of the sky over the earth to keep the waters at bay and gathered the waters under the dome together to make

Funeral Sermons that Proclaim and Celebrate

seas and for the dry land to appear. Although there are plenty of places in scripture where water is good and life giving there is always this threat in the background with the waters of chaos. I guess that is appropriate for our lives as we have plenty of good things to celebrate but there is always that doubt, that fear, that something could come and destroy our happiness. We worry about money, children, careers, our health, and death.

In the story of Noah, God opened the windows in the sky dome and let the waters of chaos in to flood the earth and wash it of all that is against God saving Noah and his family. Afterward God considered what had happened and pledged that it would never happen again. Never will God allow the waters to overtake the earth and life again. But there are still those places where the waters make themselves known. There were the waters of the Red Sea that threaten to trap the Israelites as they flee slavery in Egypt. There were the waters of the Sea of Galilee that seem ready to swamp the disciple's boat. Those same seas threatened them again as they tried to get to the other shore.

There is salvation in all these stories. God divided the Red Sea; Jesus spoke and the storm grew still; Jesus walked on the stormy waters and reached the disciples. Yet even in the midst of these salvation stories the waters are still present. They still seem to be a very real and present threat. It is only when we get to this passage from the Revelation of Saint John that we hear those wondrous words, ..."and the sea was no more.' Heaven is no longer separated from earth by the waters of chaos. That which would threaten the orderly creation of God has been banished and is gone forever. Heaven comes down to earth and God no longer sits above and separate from earth but comes and dwells with us. No more sickness. No more death. No more tears or mourning. The creation of God is fulfilled.

Today we understand the fear of the waters of chaos although we may not talk about our fear that way. We know what it is to face death with its tears and its mourning. We know the loss of the physical presence of a loved one. And we have also experienced God's acts of salvation in the life of *Name*. Where ever we have experienced love through *his/her* life, we have experienced that stilling of the waters of chaos and the presence of God's redeeming love.

We celebrate *Name's* life and the presence of God among us as we remember *his/her* life. *Name* was....

Personal reflections

We are grateful for God's acts of salvation through the love that we share together. We find it today in the presence of family and friends who mourn and cry with us; who laugh and remember with us. We look forward to that day when the waters of chaos will be gone completely and we shall gather in the presence of God and of all our loved ones. Let us continue to care for one another in the weeks and months ahead doing all we can to join God in keeping the waters of grief from overwhelming each other. Let us remember that God's plan is for a brighter day where we will bask in the sunlight of God's love forever.

www.ingramcontent.com/pod-product-compliance
Lightning Source LLC
Chambersburg PA
CBHW051717040426
42446CB00008B/928